	DATE DUE		

HOW-TO SPORTS

FOOTBALL

Paul Joseph
ABDO & Daughters

Published by Abdo & Daughters, 4940 Viking Drive, Suite 622, Edina, Minnesota 55435.

Printed in the United States.

Cover Photo credits: Allsport
Interior Photo credits: Allsport, pages 5, 9, 13, 15, 23
                        Superstock, pages 7, 11, 19, 21, 27

Edited by Bob Italia

Library of Congress Cataloging-in-Publication Data

Joseph, Paul, 1970-
    Football / Paul Joseph
      p. cm. -- (How-To-Sports)
    Includes index.
    Summary: Explains how to play football including discussion of the basic rules, the various positions, special teams, and required equipment.
      ISBN 1-56239-646-3
    1. Football—Juvenile literature. 2. Football—Terminology-Juvenile literature.
[1. Football.] I. Title. II . Series.
    GV950.7.J67 1996   95-52033
    796.332--dc20   CIP
                                                                 AC

Contents

How Football Started

Many historians believe the first football game was played by Harvard and Yale Universities in 1875. But the game did not look anything like the one played today. Rules from soccer and **rugby** were used. The two teams tried to push, kick, or shove the ball through the other team for a goal.

Yale coach Walter Camp changed the game and made many new rules. Most of his ideas are still used today. Camp reduced the number of players on each side to 11. He also invented the **huddle** to call plays.

It wasn't long before football started catching on at other colleges and became a popular sport.

Football teams huddle to call their plays.

The Basics of Football

Football games often are played on a flat field that is 100 yards (91 m) long from **goal line** to goal line, and 53 yards (48 m) wide. There is a 10-yard (9-m) area called the **end zone** behind the goal line.

The object of the game is to take the ball from any point on the field and cross the other team's goal line. This is called a **touchdown**. A touchdown is worth six points.

The **offense** is the team that has the ball and is trying to score a touchdown. The **defense** is the team that tries to stop the offense from scoring.

Football can be played by many different age groups. Young people often play touch or flag football. In touch football, you do not **tackle** the ball carrier. You only need to touch the runner to stop the play. In

flag football, each player wears a flag. To stop the
play, you grab the ball carrier's flag. Otherwise, the
same football rules still apply.

A flag football team.

The Offense

The **offense** is the team with the football. A basic offense has a **quarterback**, two **running backs**, two **receivers** and six **linemen**. The quarterback touches the ball on every play by taking the **snap** from the **center**. The quarterback will either pass, run, or **hand off** to a running back.

The running backs line up behind the quarterback. They often take the hand off from the quarterback. They also block and catch passes.

The two receivers often line up on opposite sides of the field, close to the **sidelines**. They run

Opposite page:
The running back is the
player who runs with the ball.

pass routes and catch the ball. These players are usually very fast runners.

The **linemen** stand close to each other to form a line. They block the **defense** so the **quarterback** has time to throw the ball. They also block so the **running backs** are free to run.

Tight ends are linemen that block and also go out for passes. The lineman who **hikes** the ball is called the **center**.

Opposite page:
The linemen stand very
close to each other and
form a line.

The Defense

The **defense** is the team that stands on the opposite side of the **offense**. They try to stop the offense from scoring a **touchdown** and gain control of the ball.

A basic defense has four **linemen**, four **linebackers**, two **cornerbacks**, and one **safety**.

The linemen try to stop the player who has the ball, and prevent the **quarterback** from **handing off** or throwing the football.

The four linebackers line up behind the linemen. There are two middle and two outside linebackers. They try to stop the **running backs** if

Opposite page:
These defensemen are
chasing down a running back.

the **linemen** can't. They also cover the **running backs** if they go out for passes.

The two **cornerbacks** cover each **receiver**. They try to knock down or intercept passes.

The last player on **defense** is the **safety**. This player is the last hope if the running back gets by everyone else. That's why the position is called "safety." This player also helps the cornerbacks cover the receivers.

Opposite page:
The defensive line gets
ready for the next play.

How-To
Football

Offense

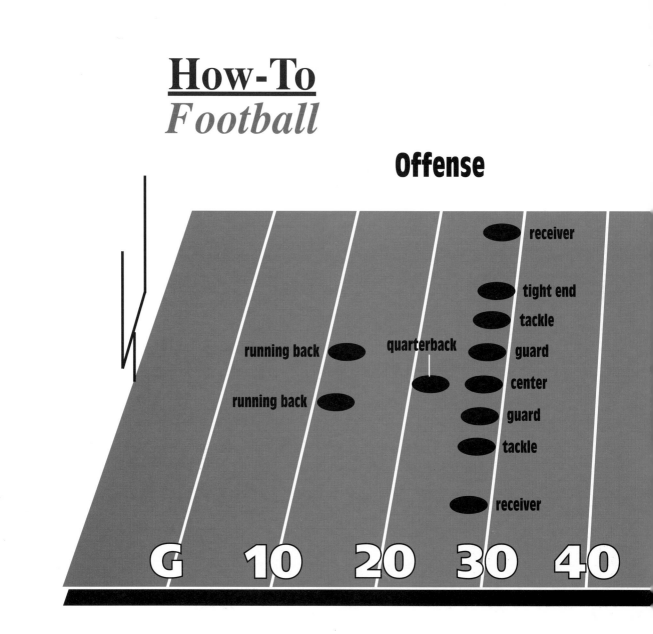

receiver

tight end

tackle

running back   quarterback   guard

center

running back   guard

tackle

receiver

G   10   20   30   40

Defense

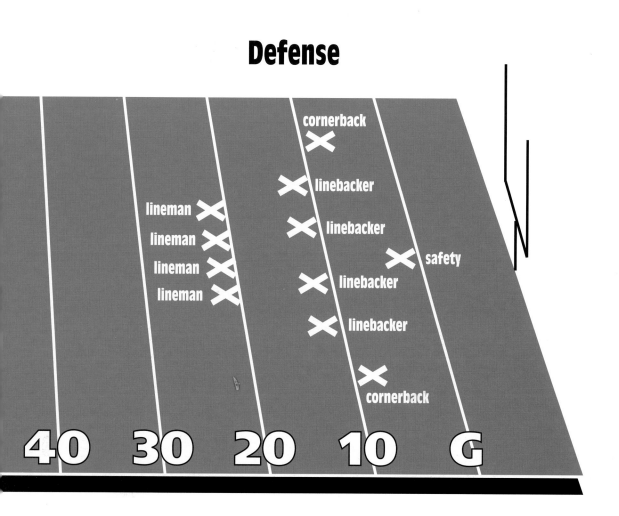

cornerback

linebacker

lineman

linebacker

lineman

lineman

safety

lineman

linebacker

linebacker

cornerback

40 30 20 10 G

Special Teams

Special teams are neither **offense** or **defense**. For example, the kickoff team is used at the beginning of the game, after a team has scored, or at the beginning of the third **quarter**.

The kickoff team lines up side-by-side with the **kicker** in the middle. The kicker boots the ball as far as possible. Then the rest of the kickoff team tries to stop the player with the ball.

The kickoff team kicks to the receiving team. One player catches the kick and tries to run without being **tackled**. The rest of the receiving team blocks for the runner.

The **punting** team is used when the offensive team doesn't think it can score a **touchdown** and must give the ball to the opponent. A punt is like a kick